INEXORABLE CONLICT OR OPPORTUNITY: THE UNITED STATES AND THE MIDDLE EAST

The Middle East, the birthplace of monotheism and of the world's three major religions – Judaism, Christianity, and Islam – has been a locus of conflict and strife for millenia. Over the last 1,200 years conflict stemmed primarily from disputes among these three great religions: their beliefs, their desire for power, their struggles for legitimacy and identity, and their cultures. Although these religions share much of the same heritage, ideals, and vision, they have not shared the same progress throughout time. Islam, founded six centuries after Christianity, continues to struggle with its identity and place in the modern world. The Middle East is the locale of this on-going struggle for Muslim identity, legitimacy, as its place in the modern world. The Christian West, including the United States, has not suffered the magnitude of setbacks that have plagued Muslims or Jews throughout history. However, the Christian West and the United States have been playing a causal role in many of the Muslim setbacks in the Middle East.

The events of September 11th, 2001 have rekindled this smoldering struggle. Ancient emotions and recent reactions have made the Middle East a flash point for global conflict. In the eyes of Middle Eastern Muslims, current issues and problems are mystically, emotionally, and eternally tied to a past that has seen the well-being of the Muslim civilization, at least in the eyes of Muslims, threatened by Western Christian advancement and progress. Such perceptions in the Muslim Middle East have precipitated resentment and disaffection toward the Christian West. These tensions have led to violence, war, and a greater divide between the three dominant world religions and their respective states.

The United States now faces the great challenge of dealing with this historic and current challenge. Violence and a continuing inability to create peace between Israel and Palestine reigns. Wars in Afghanistan and Iraq and acts of "Islamic" terror have fueled global tensions and shaken international security. The challenge for the United States, as the world's leading superpower, is to formulate a sound, effective political strategy which does not rely heavily on military power to remove the sources and conditions of Islamic extremism and to allay discontent and disaffection in the Arab world. In short, the United States and the West must acquire a greater understanding of Islam and the region in order to ease current tensions and contribute to regional stability. This cannot be achieved by ignoring history or by discounting the failures of past and present policy. Effective policy must acknowledge the complexity and real needs and desires of the Middle Eastern Muslims. The United States cannot and should not do this alone, so this strategy must be executed multilaterally. It must appear just and fair to the people of the United States, to the people of Middle Eastern states, and to the international community. The United States and its allies must understand the effects of their actions and policies on Middle Eastern Muslims. They must avoid actions and policies which tend to provoke strong resistance. They must acknowledge a modern Muslim identity which is deeply and emotionally tied to its past – a past greatly influenced by Western Christianity and U.S. policies.[1]

Brief History of Islam

The history of Islam has been presented by many clerics, historians, and scholars from many perspectives over the years. The following historic sketch

2

describes a few key points in the history of Islam in the Middle East in order to show how these significant events continue to impact the struggle for peace in the region and throughout the world today. This historic overview explains why these events hold such great emotional impact and importance for Muslims throughout the region today. For them, there is little separation in time and significance between what occurred in 610, 1095, 1258, 1920, or 1967 and today. For Middle Eastern Muslims, this deep and mystical connection between the past and present establishes their identity, underlies their well-being, and in many ways accounts for their actions.

The Middle East has been both the birthplace of valued human endeavors and a cauldron of dispute. This region gave rise to urban civilization, advanced mathematics, architecture, and literature. Modern civilization owes much of its current status and progress throughout time to this still very volatile region of the world. Maybe the region's greatest contribution to humanity, as well as the source of its ongoing volatility and conflict, is monotheism. As the birthplace of Judaism, Christianity, and Islam, the sacredness of the land from which these three major religions emerged continues to be a source of deep and complex conflict that affects the entire planet. The children of Abraham – Jews, Christians and Muslims – continue to struggle with one another, not only over religion but also in response "to political, economic, and social failures, to loss of a sense of identity, values, or meaning, to profound disillusionment or despair."[2]

Islam began its rise to power in the 7th century. Muhammad ibn Abdallah was born in 570 CE in Mecca, located in the west of what is now the Kingdom of Saudi Arabia. In 610 CE, Muhammad had the first of a series of visions in which the angel Gabriel directly revealed the word of God to him. More revelations would follow over the next twenty years. These encounters and revelations between Muhammad and the angel Gabriel are set forth in the Koran, which was compiled shortly after Muhammad's death in 632 CE.[3] Muslims regard the Koran as the precise and direct word of God; therefore, the Koran is considered infallible and absolute. The Koran is the basis for the codified laws of Islam – the Sharia. This body of laws regulates Muslim life. Muslims regard them as an expression of God's will. Nonetheless, Sharia is to be interpreted by Islamic scholars and leaders, many times these interpretations are expressed through fatwas.[4] Fatwas are formal legal opinions issued by a recognized religious legal authority. Fatwas are most frequently issued in response to questions about living everyday life in accordance with religious law, such as proper diet, gender relations, or the use of new technologies, for example. However, fatwas, in modern times, have also been used to communicate radical anti-Western messages.

After uniting all the tribes of Arabia, Muhammad became the most powerful man in the region – the leader of all Muslims. He was responsible for the Constitution of Medina, which established a federation of Islamic tribes and essentially created the first Islamic state. Medina represented the political unity of the Muslim community or Ummah. Muhammad served both as a religious prophet and political leader, so his death in 632 CE left a vacuum of both spiritual and political leadership. Muhammad was followed by the Caliphs.

Elected in 632 CE, the first caliph, Abu Bakr, established the first system of governance in Arabia. Under this system, the government represented the people and obliged them to obey Sharia. Abu Bakr's election as the first caliph marks the beginning of the split between the two main branches of Islam. The split began over a disagreement over who would lead the Ummah after Muhammad died. The side that would become the Shiite branch of Islam believed that only direct descendants of the Prophet should become caliph – the leader of the world's faithful. They were known as the Shiat-Ali, or "partisans of Ali." The Shiat-Ali believed that Muhammad's cousin and son-in-law, Ali, should be the first caliph. Over time, this group came to be known as Shiites. The other sect of Islam, the Sunnis, believed that any man deemed worthy of the position could lead the faithful, regardless of any lineage to Muhammad. For the first caliph, they favored Abu Bakr, an early convert to Islam who, as Muhammad's father-in-law, was part of Muhammad's inner circle. The term Sunni came from the Arab word for "followers"; it is a diminutive for "followers of the prophet."[5]

On his deathbed in 634 CE, Abu Bakr appointed Umar ibn al-Khattab as his successor. Umar reigned ten years and led the Muslim army that invaded and conquered most of what became the Middle East, including Iraq, Syria, Palestine, Egypt, Iran, Cyprus, Afghanistan, Sind, and portions of North Africa. Umar was assassinated in 644 CE and succeeded by Uthman ibn Haffan. Uthman, in turn, was assassinated in 656 CE by Muslim soldiers who appointed Muhammad's cousin and son-in-law, Ali ibn Abi Talib as the new caliph. However, Ali was not accepted universally as the Muslim caliph. Under Ali's rule the first Muslim civil war (fitnah) ensued, resulting in his murder in 661 CE. So in the three decades following Muhammad's death in 632 CE, a Muslim nation was established and most of what is now the Middle East was conquered and occupied. Then Muslim civil war broke out and three of the first four caliphs were assassinated within seventeen years.[6]

After Ali's death, Muawiyyah ibn Abi Sufyan, Ali's adversary, declared himself caliph. This marked the start of the Umayyad dynasty, which reigned from 661-750 CE. This first dynastic period marked the end of quasi-democratic governance, or elective monarchy, and replaced it with an essentially hereditary monarchy. Muawiyyah moved the Muslim capital from the sacred city of Medina to Damascus. The Umayyad dynasty was marked with rapid advances in territorial gains. His caliphate extended from as far as East Persia and modern Pakistan to Northern Africa, and as far west as modern Spain. As it expanded, control of the caliphate became less centralized. Then the Ummah became reluctant to accept the legitimacy of Islamic leaders outside the lineage of the descendants of Mohammad. This period was marked by numerous rebellions against the Umayyad dynasty; this unrest exploded into the second Muslim civil war in 660 CE and subsequent uprisings in Iraq and Iran. The end of the Umayyad also signaled a distinct historic split in the Ummah. As the Umayyad dynasty collapsed in 750 CE, the supporters of Banu Hashim of Mohammad's clan and descendants of Mohammad's uncle Ali split further from the Sunni majority, which deepened the split between Shia and Sunnis. This split of the sects resulted in the Abbasid dynasty, which then ruled from 750-1258 CE.[7]

The first Abbasid caliph, Abu al-Abbas al-Saffah, came to power in 750 CE; during his first four years in power, he massacred all of the members of the Umayyad family. Then an absolute Islamic monarchy was born. 762 CE marked the founding of Baghdad as capital of the new Abbasid dynasty. Under Caliphate Harun al-Rashid, the most prominent Abbasid caliph, a cultural renaissance blossomed in Baghdad and throughout the empire, as the arts and science flourished. This period also marked a further development toward a more practicable form of Sharia, or Islamic law. The capital was moved from Baghdad to Samarra in 848 CE. 935 CE marked the point at which caliphs lost political power within Islam: They retained only symbolic authority. Power now fell to local rulers, who established distinct and separate dynasties throughout the Islamic empire. Various discrete dynasties, outside the direct rule of the Abbasids, were established between the early 10th century and 1118 CE throughout Iran, Spain, Egypt, Syria, Northern India, and Turkey.[8]

In 1095 CE, Pope Urban II launched the first of many Christian Crusades, which continued until 1291 CE. In 1099 CE, crusaders occupied Jerusalem and massacred many Muslims and Jews. They also destroyed Jerusalem's mosque. This was a devastating blow to Islam. This initial Western aggression in the Middle East, and the violence associated with it, horrified the Muslim people. The Crusades produced a tragic and lasting legacy of religious conquest. In *Holy Wars*, Karen Armstrong notes the consequence of this legacy: "One holy war had continuously led to another for a hundred years, until finally it looked as though the Christians had produced the murderous cruelty and hatred that they had felt for the Muslims in the heart of the Muslims themselves."[9]

In recent times, the effect of the West becoming more powerful and threatening to the Middle East has triggered a rebirth of Islamic loathing of the West. Violent Islamic organizations have committed desperate acts of aggression to eject current modern invaders from the Middle Eastern Islamic heartland.[10] As Armstrong explains, "This is not just because 'history repeats itself' in a deterministic cycle of fate. It is because Muslims perceive a similar Western aggression which has produced a similar effect in

Muslims of the Middle East in our own times."[11] The Christian Crusades in the Middle East, at the time, had little direct effect on the greater Islamic world. Nonetheless, modern colonization, imperialism, and globalization have reawakened Muslim resentments of the Crusaders. Modern Middle Eastern Muslims, clerics, and scholars look back with nostalgia at the Islamic resistance to the first Western aggression. They yearn for a unifying Islamic leader who can resist the modern "Crusade-like" actions of the modern Western Christian world. Muslims recall a figure such as Ṣalāḥ ad-Dīn Yūsuf ibn Ayyūb (Saladin), founder of the Ayyubid dynasty and celebrated leader in Muslim history. Saladin's chivalrous resistance to and successful campaigns against the West during the Crusades, the high point of which was the Islamic recapture of Jerusalem, is the kind of mystic leader the Ummah long for at present. A true Muslim unifier, he was not only deeply revered in the Middle East but respected as a valorous Islamic figure in Europe as well.[12] Though some have attempted to fill the void left following his passing, Muslims have yet to find a unifying Islamic leader as magnanimous and dynamic as Saladin. Only by seeing the Crusades through the eyes of Muslims in modern times can anyone understand how the past lives in their eyes and dreams.[13]

In 1257, the Mongol army led by the Hulegu, the grandson of Genghis Khan, began his march on Baghdad. In 1258, following Hulegu's Siege of Baghdad, the city – capital of the Abbasid Caliphate and one of the world's great centers of learning – was pillaged and burned. Its occupants were slaughtered. Its educational and scientific achievements were in shambles. The destruction of valuable manuscripts and the slaughter of scholars in the city retarded intellectual advancement for centuries:[14]

Baghdad was one of the most brilliant intellectual centers of the world. The Mongol destruction of Baghdad was a psychological blow which Islam never recovered from. Islam was already turning inward and more conservative, becoming more suspicious of conflicts between faith and reason. The intellectual flowering of Islam was snuffed out. As a result, Baghdad remained depopulated and in ruins for several centuries, and the event is widely regarded as the end of the Islamic Golden Age. Politically and economically, the Mongol invasions were disastrous. Some regions never fully recovered and the Muslim empire, already weakened by internal pressures, never fully regained its previous power. The Mongol invasions, in fact, were a major cause of the subsequent decline that set in throughout the heartland of the Arab East. In their sweep through the Islamic world the Mongols killed or deported numerous scholars and scientists and destroyed libraries with their irreplaceable works. The result was to wipe out much of the priceless cultural, scientific, and technological legacy that Muslim scholars had been preserving and enlarging for over five hundred years.[15]

The psychological impact of Hulegu's destruction of Baghdad on Muslims was perhaps the most devastating consequence of the Mongol invasions. As Karen Armstrong asserts, "The trauma of the invasions had, not surprisingly, made Muslims feel insecure. Foreigners were not only suspect; they could be as lethal as the Mongols."[16]

The reign of the Turkish Ottoman Empire extended from 1299 to 1923; it was sustained by Islam and Islamic institutions. In the early 20th century, the Empire was internally challenged by a revolt of the "Young Turks" and externally by the onset of World War I. Dissident groups throughout the Empire challenged the rule of Sultan Abdulhamid II, and he was deposed in 1908 by reformers known as the Young Turks. They were supported by similar dissident groups throughout the Empire. Their waning allegiance to the Ottoman State eventually gave rise to "nationalists" movements throughout the Empire."[17] British strategic interest in the region also contributed to the eventual fall of the empire. "Instead of looking for ways to preserve the Ottoman Empire, Britain now contemplated the best way to carve it up."[18] As World War I came to an end, the British cleverly made promises "of postwar spoils from the carcass of the

Ottoman Empire."[19] Indeed, the end of World War I signaled the beginning of a new era in the Middle East. That new era was sealed with the Treaty of Versailles and the Treaty of Lausanne.

The Treaty of Versailles, ending World War I, stripped the Ottoman Empire of all territories outside its heartland in Anatolia and gave Greece nominal control of the coast of Asia Minor and the Ottoman's remaining European territory. The July 1923 Treaty of Lausanne was the consequence of war between the new Turkish Republic and Greece, the advancement of the modern nation-state, and the sovereignty of the new Turkish Republic. The effect of the treaty restored all of Asia Minor and portions of Thrace to Turkey, resulting in the current boundaries of the new Turkish Republic.

The Ottoman Empire was the last hegemony that sustained the concept of Muslim unity (Ummah). The collapse of the Ottoman Empire led to a period when the Ummah were divided and funneled into territorial states, which were largely created by European powers from the wreckage of the Ottoman Empire. These colonial partitions further splintered Islam into separate, independent Arab states and eventually into more than 40 modern Muslim states.[20] As a result of the fall of the Ottoman Empire, the Ummah were permanently separated and splintered into separate societies without a unified Islamic law. Islamic ideals and Islamic identity fell by the wayside of Western imperialism and global wars. The Modern Muslim state had been born; but Islam, as a nation, had been seemingly fragmented forever.[21]

The unparalleled rise of the West from the 18th century on was the next key factor in Middle Eastern Islamic history that created complex future issues. This rise led not only to modernization but also to social and intellectual growth in the West. It also promoted more tolerant, secular, and Western democratic forms of government, which enhanced social progress. The West's separation of church and state enabled scholars, scientists, and intellectuals to work free from past restrictions of religious pressures and oppressive leadership.[22] Western progress had long-term ruinous effects on the Islamic Middle East. The need for raw materials in Western societies to support rapid modernization and industrial advancement led to the colonization of much of the Middle East, Africa, and India. Colonial reactions were mixed: Some Middle Eastern Muslims grudgingly admired Western progress and organization. Nevertheless, the overarching result was that Middle Eastern Islam chose to look inward, to close out things Western.[23] Despite the efforts of some Islamic reformers, the Islamic majority were unwilling to accept or compete with Western progress. As a result, Middle Eastern Muslims became increasingly dependent on their European colonizers. Muslims were opposed to separation of church and state within Islam. As the Western world advanced, Middle Eastern Islamists returned to what they were most comfortable with – the teaching of Prophet Mohammad, the Koran, and Sharia. Muslims continue to struggle with how to live within their faith in a rapidly changing global society. Instead of embracing modernization, as the West moved forward the Middle East turned inward and looked backward to Islam. In effect, their religion provided Middle Easterners with an escapist's comfort zone. The West also failed to anticipate the consequences of colonization and Islamic resentments and loathing of Western progress. As Karen Armstrong explains:

> Muslims could easily be dismissed now as the "barbarous infidel" and the former achievements of Islam were no longer a threat and could be ignored. But it is a mistake to imagine that, because we don't see it, it no longer exists. The Arabs failed to "see" Christianity and imagined that

Europe had developed little since the period of the Crusades: at the end of the century they would get a severe shock when they encountered the new West. In our own century we in the West were shocked by the new outbreak of revolutionary Islamic activity and realized belatedly that Islam had been alive and well all along but we had not "seen" it.[24]

The passionate, mystical, emotional, and deeply religious history of the Middle East is also a critical factor in the deep and long struggle among Jews, Christians, and Muslims. This complex conflict – exacerbated by violence, political opportunism, and harsh policies – has contributed to cataclysmic and tragic events in this century.[25] History has favored the Christian West in this struggle: Its power, legitimacy, and modernization have dominated the struggle, especially in the matter of the establishment of a strong Western ally in the region – Israel.

Contemplating a reversal of this good fortune and recollection of past triumphs of Islam may bring some understanding to the present. What if the tides of history and fortune were reversed? The world today would be a profoundly different place if Christianity had been founded six centuries after Islam - if a Christian Europe had faced the destruction of Islamic Crusades in the 11th century; had endured the Mongols' destruction of its institutions of learning, culture, civilization; had been usurped by Islamic colonization and imperialism. Additionally, the world may also be significantly different today if not for certain near-misses throughout Muslim history, such as the close Islamic losses at the Siege of Constantinople (717-718) and the Battle of Tours (732) – or the near breakthrough of the Ottoman Turks at Vienna in 1529 or 1683.

If such roles were reversed and the Christian West had suffered these extreme setbacks or losses, it is not difficult to envision a Western Christian civilization lagging far behind Islamic progress, prosperity, and modernity. It is furthermore possible to envision modern Christian "jihadists" or "crusaders" conducting suicide bombing operations in Baghdad, Tehran, Damascus, and Jerusalem to counter the aggression that they perceive threatens their legitimate existence and identity. The current status of Islam in the Middle East is undoubtedly affected by its past, which certainly is clouded by Islam's internal struggle. Moreover, it has been impacted by external struggles. The Crusades, the Mongol Invasions, WWI and the fall of the Ottoman Empire, European colonization, and the rapid rise of Western civilization and the nation-state – all have left their mark on the Middle East and its Muslim populace.

Rather than resisting or embracing changes forced on them by modernity and the West, many Muslims have simply retreated to their fundamentalist religious base. They have chosen to maintain their Islamic identity and turn inward, rather than accepting the changing world and modernity. Perhaps this is the more comfortable choice. This trend continued as the US began its journey toward establishing itself as the world's sole superpower, but not without a price. That price is Middle Eastern resentment and discontent with the external powers that they will become dependent upon and discontent with.

American Hegemony, Globalization, Israel and the Middle East

The U.S. policy of decolonization following World War II, along with the creation of Israel in 1948, led to the United States emerging as a major political player in the Middle East as British and French colonial power diminished. Then, Israel's 1956 attack (with British and French support) on Egypt to prevent Egypt's nationalization of the Suez Canal prompted U.S. anger. In cooperation with the Soviet Union, the United States compelled the British, French, and Israelis to withdraw. This essentially ended British hegemonic power in the Middle East and established the United States as the "dominant Western power in the region."[26] This transfer of power had lasting consequences on the world and U.S. policy in the region. To implement its policy to contain Soviet expansion, the United States sought to establish strong political and economic relationships in the Middle East. At the same time, despite lingering tensions between the Israelis and Americans as result of the 1956 Suez Canal conflict, Israel-American relations began to improve, causing further tensions in the region. Remembering its own colonial past and struggle for independence, the United States strongly supported decolonization. U.S. advocacy of decolonization was rooted in its past and therefore a matter of principle. But this was not the only reason the United States used its influence in the United Nations to defer post-WWII decolonization efforts of its European allies. The United States was also interested in extending U.S. influence throughout the globe, both for economic interests and as a means to contain Soviet aggression in these former colonial territories and developing countries. Despite its strategic merits, this U.S. strategy was perceived in Islamic countries as a U.S. plot to replace the European colonial powers in the Middle East. As imperialism diminished and independent nation-states filled the void, U.S. hegemonic military and economic power expanded. In order to combat communism and protect and expand its global interests, the United States projected power and established military bases in Korea, Indochina, Latin America, Africa, and the Middle East in order to contain communism and establish U.S. global influence.

The U.S. and European support for the establishment of Israel through the UN, in response to the persecution of European Jews and the horror of the holocaust, had a profound effect on Middle Eastern Muslims in the region. Many Muslims charged that Israel was foisted on them to assuage Western guilt. The more subtle truth is that

Jewish immigration to Palestine started in the late 19th century as a policy of the Ottoman Empire. Jewish settlers boosted the economy of the province, which then attracted Muslim immigrants to the region. The increasingly perplexing problem of what to do about Muslims and Jews living in what Jews thought was their homeland, which they had rebuilt with the approval of the Caliphs in Istanbul, was one of issues attending the collapse of the Ottoman empire.

Within a decade of its creation, the United States embraced Israel as a major strategic partner in the Middle East.[27] This relationship has been based on shared values and histories; both are, in a sense, creations of Europe. Israel also provided a democratic model in the Middle East, an area of the world where the concept had not caught on. However, many would argue that Israel's status as a "Jewish" state and its treatment and discrimination of non-Jews belies its claims to a liberal democracy in the U.S. sense. Unfortunately, the U.S. relationship with Israel has come at the expense of its relations with much of the rest of the Middle East. The U.S. guarantee of Israeli security and US financial aid to the state, regardless of its effects on Palestine and the rest of the Arab-Muslim Middle East, has been a "misjudgment of gigantic proportions," according to Amin Saikal in his book, *Islam and the West, Conflict or Cooperation*.[28] Even so, there is no doubt that support for Israel provides a strategic benefit for the United States in the Middle East. U.S. politicians have also used support for Israel to their political advantage. But it has also fueled anti-U.S. attitudes and actions, especially among Arab Muslims in the Middle East.

Although the United States tried through diplomacy to prevent the 1967 Six Day War between Israel and a coalition of Egypt, Jordan, and Syria, U.S. support for Israel led to deep anguish and resentment from Muslims in the region. U.S. leaders feared the war could escalate, especially if the USSR was drawn into it. However, U.S. leaders failed to anticipate the immediate and future impacts of U.S. failure to deter Israeli aggression. The war ended with a swift and decisive Israeli victory. Israel then wrested control of the Gaza Strip and the Sinai Peninsula from Egypt; of the West Bank and East Jerusalem from Jordan; and of the Golan Heights from Syria. Israel thereby tripled its territory from 8,000 to 26,000 square miles and inherited more than 750,000 hostile Palestinians.[29]

Israel's annexation of East Jerusalem was not taken lightly by Muslims in the region. Opinions are still divided as to whether Israel's attack was an act of aggression or a preemptive defensive strike. But clearly Middle Eastern Muslims regarded it as an act of aggression supported by the mighty United States. It is also clear that Israel, facing a series of threatening gestures from three Arab states, felt justified in launching their pre-emptive strike against Egypt on 5 June 1967.[30] The loss of the East Jerusalem, in particular, to the U.S.-backed Isrealis created an extreme sense of humiliation and dejection. For the Middle Eastern Islamists, this was reminiscent of Muslim losses at the hands of the Crusaders and European colonialists centuries before.[31] Only a year later, President Johnson provided direct military support and a regional strategic edge to Israel through the sale of the Phantom fighter airplane to Israel. The United States could no longer sustain a posture of strategic neutrality in the Arab-Israeli conflict. Middle Eastern Muslims simply regarded the United States and Israel as allies who sought to dominate the region and oppress the displaced Palestinians.[32]

16

The Arab-Israeli and Palestinian-Israeli conflicts still play a major role in the overall Middle East Peace process. United Nations Resolutions 242 and 338, the 1993 Oslo Accords, the 2000 Camp David Summit, the 2002 "Road Map for Peace", and the 2010 Direct Talks have all been major efforts to bring some form of resolution and peace to the region. None have accomplished that goal. Israel, with U.S. support, continues to exacerbate regional issues and to complicate U.S. relations with other countries in the region. The United States is not deemed an honest broker in the matter of Arab-Israeli issues. U.S. leaders continue to tilt toward Israel as its primary ally in the Middle East. Shared U.S.-Israeli values and interests will likely ensure that the relationship will remain as it has for the past 63 years. This relationship and its anti-U.S. spin-offs will continue to complicate U.S.-Islamic Middle East relations. It surely prevents the United States from effectively brokering peace in the region.

American Image and Islamic Extremism

The long, violent and complicated history of the Middle East was brought to the forefront of the international public on September 11th, 2001. The horrible images of "9/11" cast a blinding light on the issue of "Islamic extremism." As the West and the United States began to peel back the layers of jihadist movements and Islamic extremism in order to counter its threat, it became increasingly clear that what it faced was not solely a struggle with militant Islamic extremists seeking to destroy the United States and its allies. It was equally, or more so, a struggle within Islam itself. Without doubt, the United States and the West were part of the problem. But they had also been drawn in to this complex struggle. Understanding "Islamic extremism" begins with grasping where it came from.

The godfather of radical Islam is Sayyid Qutb (1906-1966). Qutb's writings inspired future global jihadist ideology. Qutb's writings also inspired militant actions against oppressive anti-Islamic governments and the influence of United States and the USSR in the Middle East. He preached that all Muslims are obliged to combat these evils. If they refused this obligation, they were also enemies of Allah themselves.[33] The next leader of Islamic extremism was Abdullah al-Assam (1941-1989), who is considered the prince of global jihad. This university professor preached that militant jihad was the obligation of all able-bodied Muslims. He was responsible for romanticizing the concept of martyrdom or sacrificing one's life for Allah in exchange for eternal paradise. His ideology would be operationalized decades later by his follower, Osama bin Laden.[34]

Born in 1957, the educated and wealthy Saudi Osama bin Laden used the teachings and ideologies of both Qutb and al-Azzam to bring radical militant Islamic extremism to the world stage. Influenced greatly by his experience fighting the Soviets in Afghanistan in the 1980s, bin Laden created the well-known Islamic extremist terror network al-Qaeda. The U.S.-led Gulf War in 1991, in partnership with Saudi Arabia transformed bin Laden's life and led to his declaration of jihad to drive the United States out of the Middle East, to overthrow the Saudi Arabian government, and to liberate Mecca and Medina from secular control. His profound hatred for the United States and Israel led to his first 1996 fatwa which emphasized the duty of all Muslims to kill Americans and their allies anywhere in the world.[35] Bin Laden's fatwa is not considered legitimate by many Muslims. He is considered by many to be a criminal, and has no recognized religious authority. Nonetheless, Al-Qaeda has become the consummate symbol of Islamic extremism; it is responsible for global acts of terror in the United States, Europe, Indonesia and throughout the Middle East. Two major U.S.-led wars in Iraq and Afghanistan have been waged to destroy al-Qaeda.

The 9/11 al-Qaeda attacks on the United States prompted strong reactions throughout the world. In fact, strong support and sympathy for the United States emanated from some Islamic and non-Islamic states alike. The United States had an opportunity, at that moment in history, to seek both justice for the heinous acts committed against her and to unite the counter terrorist effort to her advantage. The United States missed that opportunity by not fully grasping what happened to her, why it happened, and by whom. Although the use of force was absolutely necessary and completely appropriate in order to seek out and destroy Islamic terror cells throughout the world, the United States did not appropriately calculate the enemy's enduring intent, which is deeply tied to its Islamic history, legacy, and its people – the Ummah. The United States has effectively executed the war on terror, but has failed to fully understand and execute the war of ideas. In this war, U.S. and Western modernity has collided with a Middle Eastern Muslim desire for legitimacy framed within an ancient Islamic ideal.

America, Islam and Winning the War of Ideas

The United States cannot defeat 'Islamic extremism" and terror groups such as al-Qaeda solely with force. Use of force is essential in the current war, but it certainly is not enough. The United States is winning the battle of force, but not necessarily the "war of ideas." To win the current war, the United States must improve its message and policies with the Ummah in the Middle East, not necessarily with the governments of the Middle East. The United States must clearly identify its adversary in the current war.

19

U.S. strategists must create a unified strategy across the interagency spectrum and U.S. diplomats and information teams must negotiate with Muslim leaders and engage the Muslim populace to counter the terrorist narrative. To achieve our National Security Strategy objectives, we must begin by addressing Arab and Muslim interests while trying to align them with U.S. interests. The United States must change its current approach to the "War on Terror" by delegitimizing the al-Qaeda and Islamic terror message and positively engaging the Muslim world in the Middle East. In order to accomplish this, the United States must address the true source of Muslim discontent in the region and exhibit a willingness to apply words and actions that produce real change. In the long term the United States must unequivocally demonstrate that we share a common objective: peace and stability in the region.[36]

Foreign views of the United States were generally favorable before the United States attacked Iraq in March 2003; these views grew increasingly negative during the remainder of the Bush administration and prior to the Obama administration taking office in January 2009. Between 2000 and 2005, favorable attitudes toward the United States plummeted from 74% in Britain, Germany and France and 68% in Indonesia, Turkey and Morocco to 46% and 42% respectively.[37] Middle Eastern views of al-Qaeda and its tactics declined between 2003 and 2009, but al-Qaeda still enjoys considerable support in the Muslim world.[38] Additionally, statistics show that Muslims in the Middle East want U.S. forces out of the region and approve of attacks on U.S. troops there. A large majority also believe that a U.S. policy objective is to destroy Islam.[39] Based on U.S. unpopularity abroad and al-Qaeda's residual popularity, the United States faces an enduring challenge. The cause of growing U.S. unpopularity is the absence of much-needed support in the region. Al-Qaeda's remaining popularity enables it to find recruits and acquire money and safe havens.[40] Growing U.S. unpopularity is fueled by al-Qaeda's message, although al-Qaeda's violence against fellow Muslims has alienated it from many in the region. The United States has not done enough to directly counter al-Qaeda's message and narrative and to explain why al-Qaeda or Islamic extremism is not in the interest of the Ummah. The United States must craft a message that emphasizes objective facts over al-Qaeda propaganda, but U.S. messages must not ignore the past and Middle Eastern Muslims' view of it. This strategy must promote a respectful dialogue and actions that encourage Americans and the world's Muslims to conduct a meaningful dialogue.[41]

Before 9/11, the U.S. strategy on terror relied mostly on a law enforcement approach. The objective was not necessarily to destroy the "terror network," but rather to prosecute terrorist crimes as they occurred throughout the world. The goal was to ensure order, but not to combat global terrorism. After 9/11, the strategy changed to a broader war on terrorism in which the United States enhanced security of the homeland to protect the American people while projecting its military might to disrupt and destroy terror networks and to punish the states that sponsored them. Additionally, a primary U.S. legal and moral approach was to deny legitimacy to terrorists by treating them as anything other than criminals. This was a sensible and necessary shift in strategy. It was imperative for the United States to act quickly and firmly to defend the security of our country and the values that our citizens hold dear.

Since 9/11, much of the dynamic of the international situation has changed for the worse. Following the U.S. invasion of Iraq in 2003, it became clear that this war was about more than just disrupting and destroying terror networks. Operation Iraqi Freedom (2003-2011) was perceived by many Middle Eastern Muslims as another example of U.S. aggression. Again, U.S. action brought to the surface the deep-seated emotions in many Muslims in the region regarding Western Christian Crusades and past Western and U.S. opportunism. The Bush administration's plan to export democracy to the Middle East through Iraq failed to grasp the reality that Islamic fundamentalists abhorred the concept and were willing to fight against it at high cost. However, the strategy resulted in scores of dead militant Islamists in Iraq and Afghanistan, but U.S. military operations increased animosity toward the United States and its efforts to bring about security in the Middle East. U.S. leaders had defined the war that they wanted to fight and had executed it without understanding the intention or the nature of the enemy that the United States faced and without regard for its effect on the Muslims in the region.[42] The United States failed to take the lead on strategic communications within the Muslim world. It allowed al-Qaeda to dominate the information war and disseminate its propaganda throughout the international Muslim community, where it resonated at a deeply emotional level and with great effect through its appeal to Muslim identity and the past.

> The conventional wisdom typically has it that al-Qaeda's jihadist propaganda and media activities are hugely successful within the Muslim world and that al-Qaeda is dominating the "information war," humbling America's own meager capabilities to influence Muslim attitudes. To be sure, al Qaeda's propaganda and media strategy benefit from its ability to employ various symbols and slogans of Islam and Islamism in support of its program; for instance, al-Qaeda's leaders have identified themes — the liberation of Palestine being the preeminent one — that find resonance at a deeply emotional level for much of the Muslim world. However, al-Qaeda's ideological and propaganda weaknesses are more apparent than its strength.[43]

The last sentence of the quote above reveals an opportunity for the United States in this war of ideas. If Al-Qaeda's demented approach – such as killing civilians, distorting Islamic scripture, exploiting political weaknesses, and disseminating hateful propaganda – are more apparent than their strengths, how can the United States capitalize on that? The first step to winning the war of ideas and countering the al-Qaeda narrative is to re-define the current conflict. The "war on terror," the "long war," "overseas contingency operations," combating "jihadists" are all terms that favor the al-Qaeda narrative. These terms, recent U.S. strategy, U.S. support of Middle Eastern regimes, and the current policy of perceived uncontested support to Israel are all issues that al-Qaeda has capitalized on. They resonate deeply and emotionally in the Middle Eastern Muslim world. Al-Qaeda has been able to exploit this because the United States has not been able to frame and define the current conflict to its advantage within the region. In the absence of appropriate U.S. framing of this conflict, al-Qaeda has framed it to its own advantage. Al-Qaeda continues to conduct an effective strategic communications campaign that empathizes with and speaks directly to the concerns of the Muslims in the Middle East and throughout the world. Muslims may not agree with the tactics of al-Qaeda, but they generally agree with the ideology and principles conveyed in al-Qaeda's message. Current U.S. policy and strategy do not address, confront, or counter these issues effectively. In many cases, Muslim populations, not aligned with al-Qaeda's ideology, have not been cultivated by the United States. Instead, they have been alienated.[44] The United States has unwittingly framed this war of ideas on the enemy's terms by accepting al-Qaeda's definitions and using its terminology. This has only validated the enemy's ideological worldview by affirming the appearance that the United States has declared war on Islam.[45] In order to counter this al-Qaeda message effectively, U.S. leaders must redefine the current war against al-Qaeda and terrorism.

Al-Qaeda's goals are to drive Americans out of Muslim nations and to deny U.S. influence in Muslim nations, to destroy Israel, to topple pro-Western regimes around the Middle East, and to unite all Muslims by establishing an Islamic nation. So it must overturn the status quo in the Middle East in order to carry out its own political agenda, which is to establish an Islamic nation that adheres to the rule of the first Caliphs, which legitimizes al-Qaeda's cause. In order to accomplish this, they must win the hearts and minds of the Muslim people by means of an effective propaganda campaign. Al-Qaeda also relies on protraction of the conflict as a strategy to wait out the established regimes and governments that currently control their target population. Lastly, they use unconventional guerilla tactics and strategies to exploit their enemy's weaknesses and further legitimize their cause. By definition, the current conflict is an insurgency. This insurgency resides within Islam, not just through al-Qaeda and the Islamic extremist movements, but also through the Ummah it seeks to overthrow established regimes and implement al-Qaeda's political agenda. This insurgency is generally supported by the Ummah and calls for universal change within Islam. Even insurgent movements that operate within national societies, exampled by the current "Arab Awakening," believe their own struggle is part of a greater Islamic struggle against the status quo. Whether it is al-Qaeda or the Ummah, the United States needs to work toward understanding them, because they represent both authority and change within Islam, a change that will happen with or without the support or resistance of the United States.[46]

The U.S. strategy thus far has proven unable to address issues that the insurgency is exploiting. However, issues beyond the narrow al-Qaeda agenda are affecting the Muslim population throughout the Middle East and North Africa. Tyrannical dictators, human rights violations, government corruption, economic woes, unemployment, extreme poverty, and high percentages of disaffected educated youth within the population are some of the driving factors behind this "civilizational insurgency". By not seeing this conflict as a unique Islamic civilizational insurgency and by failing to understand its true nature and causes, U.S. efforts have proven futile and counterproductive. This insurgency calls for universal change within Islam. It is being exploited by terrorists. But it also enjoys popular support from Muslims who passively or aggressively support these insurgent fighters. This popular support provides the political basis for the Islamic terror networks.[47] The United States and its allies have focused too much on the symptoms of terrorism, such as al-Qaeda, and too little time on its root causes. The United States must acknowledge that Islamic law and tradition broadly legitimate this insurgency. Then U.S. strategy should drive a wedge between illegitimate al-Qaeda goals and actions and the Ummah's desire for legitimate change in the region. By failing to counter the al-Qaeda narrative, the United States has chosen, either intentionally or unintentionally, to oppose change within Islam. This passive strategy manifests as support to the regimes that resist and repress change. To prevail, the United States must accept this insurgency and support the legitimate change it seeks. To achieve the goal of a lasting peace and sustained security in the Middle East and throughout the globe, U.S. strategy must support the parties that shape this goal. This strategy would better position the United States on the side of the Ummah; it would support their desires and goals, and they would likely perceive it as being more supportive of their desires and goals.[48] The U.S. message and actions should speak to the Muslim people of the Middle East and show support for their desire for change. But U.S. strategy should also clearly distinguish between the legitimate goals of the people and the illegitimate desires of al-Qaeda and any other violent Islamic extremist groups.

Islamic Civilizational Insurgency

The United States must continue to disrupt and destroy terror networks that purport to support this Islamic insurgency. But U.S. strategy should seek broader objectives. Disruption and destruction of insurgency fighters must be part of a grander U.S. strategy. The United States must do more. Michael Vlahos explains in his thought-provoking article *Terror's Mask: Insurgency within Islam* that doing more means finding the root causes of this insurgency and grasping the necessity of bringing change to Islam. A U.S. strategy of intentionally bringing or supporting change within Islam could be an inherently risky one. As Vlahos suggests, U.S. involvement in bringing change to Islam raises two conditions: (1) introduced change could not be controlled, and (2) once introduced, change in the Muslim World would tend toward revolution and the eventual fall of the *"ancien regime"*.[49] Vlahos suggests that the United States should let change happen in Islam, then poise itself to deal with the new Muslim world in the Middle East. This path would relieve the United States of its current perceived "crusader" role. Then, after the revolution has culminated, it would give the United States "real" states to deal with.[50] Allowing change to happen does not mean the United States has no role in the outcome of this change. The United States now has the opportunity to work with the citizens of Tunisia, Egypt, Syria, Libya, and many of the other Arab countries whose protests have been subdued to help advance and safeguard democracy and to shape these countries' democratic reforms.

The recent events of the "Arab Spring" are undoubtedly significant. They may portend some confirmation of Vlahos' predictions. It is too early to tell. Autocratic governments, in any form, are not suited to a global community committed to values of democracy and equality. The United States should welcome democratic reforms in the Middle East that may emerge from this political movement. It should also reconsider its current support of autocracies and the Muslim populations that they repress. However, so far the United States neither predicted this movement nor took advantage of it. As a values-based society, the United States is obliged to promote democratic values throughout the world. As change occurs in the Middle East, the United States should not expect new regimes to adopt democratic governments modeled after and necessarily openly friendly to ours. Perhaps longer-term U.S. plans should anticipate such a favorable eventuality. A renewed emphasis on Middle Eastern allies and partnerships with legitimate, though not necessarily initially overtly pro-American, governments is a start point. That start point must undergird policy that aligns U.S. values with U.S. actions, not just words. According to Grant Highland,

> In any event, if a cultural shift within Islam is going to take place, it is going to have to be coincident with a political shift in Washington. The time has come where the status quo is no longer adequate for the vital interests of the people of the Middle East or America. Indeed, vital U.S. interests should necessarily shift away from resources and encompass those very people just mentioned in a vigorous struggle for their hearts, minds, and souls. Only then can lasting peace and true victory be declared.[51]

This proposed strategy must patiently support the long-term goal of general democratic reform throughout the Middle East and Northern Africa. This strategy, as pointed out by Vlahos, poses considerable risks and uncertainties. Aggressive cooperation, diplomacy, and economic support must be offered to those states that support movement toward reform, that support humane treatment of their people, that abide by international rule of law, and that offer a vision of a better future.

By aiding states such as Kuwait, Bahrain, Morocco, Jordan, Yemen, and the citizens of other states affected by the Arab Spring, the United States is positioned to attack the Islamic terrorist ideology's center of gravity, disaffected Muslims throughout the world. A passive approach of allowing Middle Eastern revolution by disaffected Muslims and possible self-implosion may enable these troubled people to discover their own version of Islamic revival within the modern world.[52] By supporting these states and their populations, the United States can assist them in discovering their own political future within the parameters of a peaceful Islam. Cautiously supporting these movements with all elements of U.S. national power could extend the on-going Arab Spring and encourage positive democratic reform throughout the region. Additionally, non-intrusive U.S. support could help to defuse the hate-filled ideology of al Qaeda and diminish its appeal to Middle Eastern Muslim populations.[53] Focusing on this center of gravity may be the best approach for disarming radical Islam. A successful Islamist revolution driven by the valid aspirations of the Middle Eastern Muslim people may effectively eliminate the support base that al-Qaeda and radical Islam currently enjoy.[54] Without this support base, the movement may consign al-Qaeda and other terrorist groups to irrelevance, thereby minimizing or eliminating a palpable global threat.

The Way Ahead

The United States and its allies, in order to effectively fight the war on terror in the future, must shift their primary focus from the symptoms of terrorism to the root causes of terror and Muslim discontent.[55] Physical destruction of al-Qaeda or any terror network does not destroy its ideology or alter the sympathetic views of those who relate to its cause. It is clear that the United States can longer ignore the needs of Muslims in the Middle East. U.S. strategy must address the effects that history has had on the Ummah. This requires that Western leaders understand that religion, culture, and government cannot be separated for the Ummah. Islam is tied intimately into everything Muslim Arabs do and think. Only a deeper understanding of Islamic culture will enable those efforts by the United States and the West to shape Middle Eastern Muslim affairs. Current U.S. strategy, policy, and military operations are causing deeper resentment and further resistance from the Ummah. [56] As explained by Amin Saikal in *Islam and the West*:

> The Muslims can only move in the direction of better understanding and reconciliation on two conditions: if the USA and its allies restructure their geopolitical interests to allow (and even help) the Muslims achieve what they need to do domestically; and if they recognize the fact that Islam is not there for them to make and remake according to their interests.[57]

How should the U.S. government approach this complex issue? The U.S. government needs to publicly re-define the current conflict throughout much of the Middle East and Northern Africa as an "Islamic civilizational insurgency." The United States should support the Muslim people's aspirations for change in the Middle East in pursuit of democracy. U.S. strategic communication should unequivocally disclose that violent extremism, as exercised by al-Qaeda, is not the way to achieve desired change toward stable democratic reforms in the Middle East. U.S. policy in the region should shift to operationalize President Obama's 2009 Cairo speech to the Muslim world.[58] He pledged that the United States would openly work with any individual or movement that is willing to confront violent extremism. Further, the United States would support transparent government and human rights and freedoms, religious freedoms, women's rights, modernization, and globalization. Finally, the United States would uphold fundamental democratic values.[59]

This option is risky: The United States may have minimal control over the outcome of revolutions in Middle Eastern and North African countries where the people are protesting. This option does not directly address the Israeli-Palestinian issue, but it may create a more democratic environment and tolerant climate over time to facilitate a more practicable and reasonable resolution. Creation of an interagency task force to quickly evaluate and plan for a way ahead that supports legitimate revolution in Middle East and North Africa to cast off autocratic and repressive regimes may minimize this risk. Additionally, the United States should re-evaluate current relationships with some current regimes, such as Saudi Arabia. This option will take time. It may take years to assess how U.S. support of legitimate revolution in the region has worked, to determine whether it supports U.S. vision of a democratic and peaceful Middle East. Nonetheless, the potential long-term positive effects of alleviating the sources of Muslim discontent are high. This option is proactive, not merely words. It has the potential to place the United States in a positive position, thus to enhance its image. It could minimize or eliminate the effects and legitimacy of terror networks that currently manipulate the Muslim population. This option offers the opportunity to adequately address the need to confront long-term Muslim opposition to United States and Western policies in the region, although it risks being perceived as more U.S. meddling in regional affairs. The suitability of this option is high: It accords with U.S. principles and values; it directly supports the initiatives and vision as described in the President's 2009 Cairo speech.

This proposal assumes a favorable settlement of the Israeli-Palestinian conflict, which is a complicated, seemingly unsolvable 60-year problem. The Israelis and Palestinians still need to negotiate solutions to the difficult issues of final borders, the status of Jerusalem, the right of Palestinian refugees to return, and the official recognition of both Israel and Palestine. This has been an intractable problem for over four decades. Israel has violated many UN resolutions, even though the UN created the state. A just resolution will require that the United States play a tough hand with their good friend and strategic partner, the Israelis. The pre-1967 Seven Day War borders, designated in UN Resolution 242, should be honored. This is unnerving to the Israelis. But the borders must be honored in a manner that enables Israel to defend itself. The state of Israel must also be recognized by the 57 Arab states within the UN that currently do not recognize them. The state of Palestine must also be recognized internationally. The United States cannot play a legitimate role in promoting transparent, legitimate and pluralistic democratic-style governments in the Middle East and throughout the world without also recognizing Palestine as state. The two-state solution would be similar to the one the Palestinians were offered in 1948 and at Camp David in 2000, which the Palestinians then refused. Saikal explains how Israel will benefit from such a solution: "Israel must be made to understand that ultimately its peace and security are intertwined with those of the Palestinian state, and without a viable independent Palestinian state there can be no peace and security for Israel."[60]

Conclusion

The Middle East is a complicated region with a complex and distressing history. Religion is the basis for much of that complication. Islam is a challenged religion and nation, and the Ummah are trying to find their way and place is this fast-paced

31

globalized world. In many cases throughout history, the West has used the Islamic people and passed them by. Middle Eastern Muslims continue to search for their identity in this modern world, but they will not let go of their past. Nonetheless, they want what all people want. U.S. and Western support of Middle Eastern regimes have neglected or denied these basic wants; Western leaders have not helped the Ummah in their quest for an Islamic identity in this modern world. Simon W. Murden expresses the problem nicely:

> The Muslim world saw enormous and unsettling events in the 20th century. The Ottoman Empire finally faded into history. European colonialism came and went. Israeli colonialism came and stayed. Nationalists led the way to independence but were tarnished by a troubled modernization and by military defeat at the hands of Israel. The oil boom made some wealthy but more frustrated. Muslims were drawn into the Cold War, while its end left the United States as an unrivaled hegemonic power. Muslims sought comfort in tradition, and the Islamic revival came to dominate the politics and culture of Muslims lands, but it did not significantly improve the lot of most Muslims. When in power, the performance of Islamists was poor. When in opposition, Islamic activism led to a paralyzed politics that went nowhere.[61]

Murder concludes, "In the absence of a great Islamic hegemon restoring the" Ummah, it is unlikely that much will change for Middle Eastern Muslims in the next few decades.[62] But the unfolding Arab Spring may be a good start.

For much of Islam's history it has been in a state of actual or cold war with the Christian West.[63] It is imperative that the United States and its allies not conduct this current war on terror with the "mindset that insists that everything else be subordinated to the requirements of success in this war..."[64] During the Cold War, the United States created geopolitical relationships that met their immediate goals of victory over the USSR, but in doing so created Realpolitik relationships that were not subordinate to its values. It is imperative that the United States not fall into this again without understanding the long-term effects of such accommodation. Since the end of World War II, the United States has upheld and backed traditionalist dictatorial regimes to ensure U.S. dominance in the Middle East.[65] The West is now forced to deal with the effects of those decisions and the fact that the citizens within those regimes are not satisfied with their opposed situation or with the United States, which got them there.

Islam has its responsibility in this current civilizational insurgency, as well. The Islamic ideal would be the reunification of the Ummah under an appropriate Islamic government.[66] Modernity, globalization, creation of the modern state, and internal strife within Islam render that ideal unachievable. Simon W. Murden claims that "In short, modern states could not really tolerate independent religious authority either in the domestic or international setting."[67] Non-Western societies generally acknowledge that the West has created a modern world that they still dominate. Nonetheless, Islamic culture continues to make Muslims struggle more with this reality than others.[68] Samuel Huntington offers a solution, "In the end, the only real option for Muslims in the 21st century is to make a better accommodation with the future rather than the past."[69] Nonetheless, "the Muslim world lives in the shadow of the vastly more advanced West, and it is widely believed by Muslims to be indifferent or hostile to their development or welfare. Scratch the surface, and most Muslims (are) unhappy about the world."[70] Frustration and rebellion are then inevitable. But can Middle Eastern Muslims use that frustration and rebellion in order to create positive and lasting change that results in prosperity and peace? Making that "better accommodation with the future rather than the past" would be a good start.[71]

The way ahead proposed in this SRP is not simple and certainly not a short term solution. To achieve some sense of victory (or achievement) in this current conflict, the United States must clarify its message and improve its policies toward Muslims in the Middle East. It must re-examine its current policies and relationships with current Middle Eastern regimes that do not reflect our values and that suppress their people. The West and the United States must acquire a greater understanding of Middle Eastern Muslims, their history, and their intimate and eternal tie to Islam. The people of the Middle East want opportunity. They want the freedom to pursue their dreams: dreams of education, economic prosperity, freedom to express themselves, freedom to practice their religion, and freedom to raise their families with the possibility of more opportunity than they had. In order for the people to accomplish this, they must create transparent, pluralistic, representative Middle Eastern governments of the people and for the people. These governments do not have to look like American democracy, but they must be based on basic democratic principles. They may appear to be overtly Islamic; there may be no separation of church and state. That may be acceptable. But, they must be tolerant of other religions and ethnicities. Democracy in the Middle East must develop from the grassroots. In the Muslim world this cannot be accomplished independently of Islam. It must be achieved in conjunction with Islam.[72]

The United States must also re-brand this current war in its favor. It must demonstrate that it is not at war with Islam. It must legitimate desired change in the Muslim world. It must attend to the democratic and values-based desires of the Muslim population in the Middle East and North Africa. It must counter the extremist narrative to achieve the strategic objective of a better peace in the Muslim world. The United

States must display its values through its actions, not solely through words. The United States needs to generally discredit Islamic extremism and separate the extremists' message, intents, and actions from the valid and legitimate desires and goals of the Ummah. Through effective engagement and policy for the region, the United States must confront, counter, and change the conditions that fueled Islamic extremism and widespread anti-Americanism in the Middle East.

Endnotes

[1] Aiman Sakal, *Islam and the West Conflict or Cooperation,* (New York: Palgrave Macmillan, 2003) 87

[2] John Esposito, *The Future of Islam,* (New York: Oxford University Press, 2010) 96

[3] Ellen Lust, ed., *The Middle East,* (Washington D.C.: CQ Press, 2011) 182

[4] Ibid.

[5] Dan Murphy, "Islam's Sunni-Shiite Split," January 17, 2007, http://www.csmonitor.com/2007/0117/p25s01-wome.html (accessed January 10, 2012)

[6] Karen Armstrong, *Islam, A Short History* (New York: Modern Library, 2000) 122

[7] Ibid.

[8] Karen Armstrong, *Holy Wars, The Crusades and Their Impact on Today's World* (New York: Anchor Books, 2001) 310

[9] Ibid., 453

[10] Ibid., 453

[11] Ibid., 453

[12] Ibid., 253

[13] Karen Armstrong, *Islam, A Short History* (New York: Modern Library, 2000) 179

[14] Steven Dutch, "The Mongols," August 27, 1998, http://www.uwgb.edu/dutchs/WestTech/xmongol.htm (accessed 30 December 2011)

[15] Ibid.

[16] Karen Armstrong, *Islam, A Short History* (New York: Modern Library, 2000) 103

[17] Ellen Lust, ed., *The Middle East* (Washington D.C.: CQ Press, 2011) 25

[18] Ibid., 25

[19] Ibid., 28

[20] Simon W. Murdern, *Islam, the Middle East and the New Global Hegemony* (Boulder, CO: Lynne Rienner, 2002) 188

[21] Ibid., 189

[22] Karen Armstrong, *Islam, A Short History* (New York: Modern Library, 2000) 142, 143

[23] Karen Armstrong, *Holy Wars, The Crusades and Their Impact on Today's World* (New York: Anchor Books, 2001) 483.

[24] Ibid., 486

[25] Ibid., xvi

[26] Ellen Lust, ed., *The Middle East* (Washington D.C.: CQ Press, 2011) 48

[27] Aiman Sakal, *Islam and the West Conflict or Cooperation,* (New York: Palgrave Macmillan 2003) 89

[28] Ibid., 89

[29] Mitchell G. Bard, *The Complete Idiots Guide to Middle East Conflict, 3rd Edition* (New York: Penguin Group, 2005) 202

[30] Karen Armstrong, *Holy Wars, The Crusades and Their Impact on Today's World* (New York: Anchor Books, 2001) 276

[31] Aiman Sakal, *Islam and the West Conflict or Cooperation,* (New York:Palgrave Macmillan 2003) 89

[32] Mitchell G. Bard, "The 1968 Sale of the Phantom Jets to Israel," http://www.jewishvirtuallibrary.org/jsource/US-Israel/phantom.html (accessed December 30, 2011)

[33] John Esposito, *The Future of Islam* (New York: Oxford University Press, 2010) 69

[34] Ibid., 68-69

[35] Ibid., 71

[36] Peter Krause and Stephen Van Evera, "Public Diplomacy: Ideas for the War of Ideas," September 2009, htttp://belfercenter.ksg.harvard.edu/files/

9.2009.Public%20Diplomacy.Ideas%20for%20the%20War%20of%20Ideas.pdf (accessed November 11, 2011)

[37] Ibid.

[38] Pew Research Center Publications, September 2009, http://pewresearch.org/pubs/1338/declining-muslim-support-for-bin-laden-suicide-bombing (accessed December 1, 2011)

[39] Dan Murphy, "Poll: Muslims show only partial support for Al Qaeda's Agenda," April 2007, http://www.csmonitor.com/2007/0425/p01s04-wome.html, (accessed December 1, 2011)

[40] Peter Krause and Stephen Van Evera, "Public Diplomacy: Ideas for the War of Ideas," September 2009, htttp://belfercenter.ksg.harvard.edu/files/9.2009.Public%20Diplomacy.Ideas%20for%20the%20War%20of%20Ideas.pdf (accessed November 11, 2011)

[41] Ibid.

[42] Michael Vlahos, "Terror's Mask: Insurgency within Islam," May 2002, http://www.5jt.com/extracts/terrorsmask.pdf (accessed November 1, 2011)

[43] Eric V. Larson, "Beyond the Shadow of 9/11," Summer 2011, http://www.rand.org/publications/randreview/issues/2011/summer/shadow3.html (accessed November 11, 2001)

[44] Scott Cullinane, "The World Hears Us," March 6, 2011, http://smallwarsjournal.com/blog/journal/docs-temp/693-cullinane.pdf (accessed November 11, 2011)

[45] Ibid.

[46] Michael Vlahos, "Terror's Mask: Insurgency within Islam," May 2002, http://www.5jt.com/extracts/terrorsmask.pdf_(accessed November 1, 2011)

[47] Ibid.

[48] Scott Cullinane, "The World Hears Us," March 6, 2011, http://smallwarsjournal.com/blog/journal/docs-temp/693-cullinane.pdf (accessed November 11, 2011)

[49] Michael Vlahos, "Terror's Mask: Insurgency within Islam," May 2002, http://www.5jt.com/extracts/terrorsmask.pdf_(accessed November 1, 2011)

[50] Ibid.

[51] Grant R. Highland, "New Century, Old Problems: The Global Insurgency within Islam and the Nature of the War on Terror," http://www.au.af.mil/au/awc/awcgate/ndu/highland.htm (accessed November 10, 2011)

[52] Ibid.

[53] Ibid.

[54] Michael Vlahos, "Terror's Mask: Insurgency within Islam," May 2002, http://www.5jt.com/extracts/terrorsmask.pdf (accessed November 1, 2011)

[55] Aiman Sakal, *Islam and the West Conflict or Cooperation,* (New York: Palgrave Macmillan, 2003) 129

[56] Ibid., 131

[57] Ibid., 135

[58] Eric Patterson, "The Arab Spring versus Cairo," November 4, 2011, http://www.foreignpolicyjournal.com/2011/11/04/the-arab-spring-vs-cairo/ (accessed January 30, 2012)

[59] U.S. Department of State Website, "Keynote Address at the National Democratic Institute's 2011 Democracy Awards Dinner," November 7, 2011, http://www.state.gov/secretary/rm/2011/11/176750.htm (accessed January 11, 2012)

[60] Aiman Sakal, *Islam and the West Conflict or Cooperation,* (New York:Palgrave Macmillan, 2003) 142

[61] Simon W. Murdern, *Islam, the Middle East and the New Global Hegemony* (Boulder, CO: Lynne Rienner, 2002) 205-206

[62] Ibid., 195

[63] Karen Armstrong, *Holy Wars, The Crusades and Their Impact on Today's World* (New York: Anchor Books, 2001) 366

[64] Aiman Sakal, *Islam and the West Conflict or Cooperation,* (New York: Palgrave Macmillan, 2003) 139

[65] Ibid., 136

[66] Simon W. Murdern, *Islam, the Middle East and the New Global Hegemony* (Boulder, CO: Lynne Rienner, 2002) 187

[67] Ibid., 188

[68] Ibid., 207

[69] Ibid., 208

[70] Ibid., 186

[71] Ibid., 208

[72] Aiman Sakal, *Islam and the West Conflict or Cooperation,* (New York: Palgrave Macmillan, 2003) 128